KRAFT

Stove Top Recipes

Publications International, Ltd.

Photography on pages 4, 18, 24, 80, 100, 104, 118, 120, 126, 132, 134, and 136 by StudioSide Photography.

Photographer: Tate Hunt
Photographer's Assistant: Jeremy Ruiz
Prop Stylist: Tom Hamilton
Food Stylists: Carol Smoler, Josephine Orba
Assistant Food Stylist: Jill Kaczanowski

Pictured on the front cover: Traditional Chicken Stuffing *(page 11)*.

Pictured on the back cover: Savory Apple Stuffing *(page 19)*.

ISBN-13: 978-1-4127-9918-8

ISBN-10: 1-4127-9918-X

Library of Congress Control Number: 2009924941

Manufactured in China.

87654321

Microwave Cooking: Microwave ovens vary in wattage. Use the cooking times as guidelines and check for doneness before adding more time.

Preparation/Cooking Times: Preparation times are based on the approximate amount of time required to assemble the recipe before cooking, baking, chilling, or serving. These times include preparation steps such as measuring, chopping, and mixing. The fact that some preparations and cooking can be done simultaneously is taken into account. Preparation of optional ingredients and serving suggestions is not included.

For consumer inquiries, call Kraft Foods Consumer Helpline at 800/431-1001.

Contents

For complete nutritional information, please visit www.kraftfoods.com.

Simply Stuffing

THESE CLASSIC RECIPES ARE THE PERFECT ACCOMPANIMENT TO ANY MEAL

spinach-mushroom stuffing

PREP: 10 min. | TOTAL: 10 min. | MAKES: 6 servings.

▶ what you need!

1 pkg. (6 oz.) STOVE TOP Stuffing Mix for Chicken

1 cup packed baby spinach leaves

1 cup sliced fresh mushrooms

2 green onions, sliced

▶ make it!

1. **PREPARE** stuffing as directed on package, adding spinach and vegetables with the stuffing mix.

   SPECIAL EXTRA:
   Sprinkle with 2 slices crumbled cooked OSCAR MAYER Bacon before serving.

apple cranberry pecan stuffing

PREP: 10 min. | TOTAL: 15 min. | MAKES: 8 servings.

▶ what you need!

1½ cups apple juice

2 Tbsp. butter or margarine

1 small apple, chopped

½ cup cranberries

1 pkg. (6 oz.) STOVE TOP Stuffing Mix for Chicken

¼ cup PLANTERS Pecan Pieces, toasted

▶ make it!

1. **BRING** juice and butter to boil in medium saucepan on high heat. Stir in apples, cranberries and stuffing mix; cover.

2. **REMOVE** from heat. Let stand 5 min.

3. **STIR** in nuts.

SUBSTITUTE:
Prepare using dried cranberries.

FEEDING A CROWD:
Prepare as directed, doubling all ingredients.

cranberry and toasted walnut stuffing

PREP: 5 min. | TOTAL: 10 min. | MAKES: 8 servings.

▸ what you need!

1⅓ cups water

½ cup dried cranberries

2 Tbsp. margarine or butter

1 pkg. (6 oz.) STOVE TOP Stuffing Mix for Chicken

½ cup coarsely chopped PLANTERS Walnuts, toasted

▸ make it!

1. **BRING** water, cranberries and margarine to boil in large saucepan.

2. **STIR** in stuffing mix; cover. Remove from heat; let stand 5 min.

3. **FLUFF** with fork. Stir in nuts.

SUBSTITUTE:
Substitute dried cherries or raisins for the cranberries.

SPECIAL EXTRA:
Sprinkle with chopped fresh parsley, sage or rosemary just before serving.

traditional chicken stuffing

PREP: 5 min. | TOTAL: 15 min. | MAKES: 6 servings.

▶ what you need!

  1 pkg. (6 oz.) STOVE TOP Stuffing Mix for Chicken

  ¼ cup chopped onions, cooked

  ¼ cup chopped celery, cooked

▶ make it!

1. **PREPARE** stuffing mix as directed on package, adding onions and celery with the stuffing mix.

   SUBSTITUTE:
   Prepare using STOVE TOP Stuffing Mix for Turkey.

baked cheese-stuffing casserole

PREP: 5 min. | TOTAL: 30 min. | MAKES: 8 servings.

▶ what you need!

2 cups water

1 Tbsp. margarine or butter

1 pkg. (6 oz.) STOVE TOP Savory Herbs Stuffing Mix

1 egg, beaten

¾ cup KRAFT Mexican Style Finely Shredded Four Cheese, divided

▶ make it!

HEAT oven to 375°F.

1. **BRING** water and margarine to boil in large saucepan. Stir in stuffing mix; cover. Remove from heat; let stand 5 min.

2. **STIR** egg and ½ cup cheese into stuffing mixture until blended. Spoon into greased 9-inch pie plate. Sprinkle with remaining cheese.

3. **BAKE** 20 min. or until casserole is heated through and cheese is melted.

SPECIAL EXTRA:
For a more rounded side dish, stir ¾ cup cooked broccoli florets or chopped cooked mixed vegetables into stuffing mixture before spooning into pie plate.

SUBSTITUTE:
Prepare using KRAFT Mexican Style 2% Milk Finely Shredded Four Cheese.

sausage and sweet potato stuffing

PREP: 10 min. | TOTAL: 30 min. | MAKES: 8 servings.

▶ what you need!

½ lb. pork sausage

1 can (16 oz.) whole sweet potatoes in syrup, undrained

1 cup water

1 pkg. (6 oz.) STOVE TOP Cornbread Stuffing Mix

▶ make it!

HEAT oven to 350°F.

1. **BROWN** sausage in large skillet on medium-high heat. Meanwhile, drain potatoes, reserving syrup.

2. **ADD** water and reserved syrup to sausage; bring to boil. Slice potatoes. Add to sausage mixture with stuffing mix; stir just until moistened. Spoon into 1½-qt. casserole; cover.

3. **BAKE** 20 min. or until heated through.

SERVING SUGGESTION:
Serve with your favorite cooked lean meat and steamed vegetables.

SUBSTITUTE:
Try with turkey sausage instead of pork.

corn and sausage stuffing

PREP: 10 min. | TOTAL: 40 min. | MAKES: 8 servings.

▸ what you need!

½ lb. pork sausage

1⅔ cups hot water

1 pkg. (10 oz.) frozen corn, thawed, drained

1 pkg. (6 oz.) STOVE TOP Cornbread Stuffing Mix

▸ make it!

HEAT oven to 350°F.

1. **BROWN** sausage in skillet; drain, reserving ¼ cup drippings.

2. **MIX** sausage, reserved drippings, hot water and corn in 1½-qt. casserole. Stir in stuffing mix just until moistened. Cover.

3. **BAKE** 30 min. or until heated through.

SHORTCUT:
To quickly thaw frozen corn, microwave for half the microwave-cooking time listed on the package. This should thaw the corn without cooking it.

CHECKING CASSEROLE DONENESS:
To check a casserole for doneness, insert a clean food thermometer into the center of the casserole. When the thermometer registers 165°F, the casserole is done.

savory apple stuffing

PREP: 5 min. | TOTAL: 15 min. | MAKES: 6 servings.

▶ what you need!

1 pkg. (6 oz.) STOVE TOP Stuffing Mix for Pork

1 apple, chopped

¼ cup cooked chopped onions

▶ make it!

1. **PREPARE** stuffing as directed on package, adding apples and onions with the stuffing mix.

ratatouille stuffing

PREP: 15 min. | TOTAL: 45 min. | MAKES: 6 servings.

▸ what you need!

2 Tbsp. oil

1 onion, chopped

6 mushrooms, quartered

1 small eggplant, cut into ½-inch cubes

1 zucchini, cut lengthwise in half, thinly sliced

1 can (14½ oz.) diced tomatoes, undrained

1 can (8 oz.) tomato sauce

2 cups STOVE TOP Stuffing Mix for Chicken in the Canister

▸ make it!

1. **HEAT** oil in large saucepan on medium-high heat. Add onions and mushrooms; cook and stir 5 min. or until tender.

2. **ADD** eggplant, zucchini, tomatoes and tomato sauce; mix well. Bring to boil; cover. Simmer on medium-low heat 15 to 20 min. or until vegetables are tender.

3. **STIR** in stuffing mix just until moistened. Remove from heat. Let stand, covered, 5 min.

NOTE:
To reduce the bitterness that eggplant sometimes has, spread eggplant cubes in single layer on paper towels; sprinkle generously with salt. Cover with additional paper towels. Let stand at least 30 min.; rinse. Drain; pat dry.

Breakfast
& Brunch

SWEET AND SAVORY WAYS TO START THE DAY

easy brunch bake

PREP: 15 min. | TOTAL: 55 min. | MAKES: 8 servings.

▶ what you need!

1 pkg. (6 oz.) STOVE TOP Stuffing Mix for Chicken

3 cups fat-free milk

1 red bell pepper, chopped

1 pkg. (10 oz.) frozen chopped spinach, thawed, squeezed dry

1 cup KRAFT 2% Milk Shredded Sharp Cheddar Cheese

2 whole eggs

2 egg whites

4 slices OSCAR MAYER Bacon, cooked, crumbled

▶ make it!

HEAT oven to 350°F.

1. **COMBINE** ingredients.

2. **SPOON** into greased 13×9-inch baking dish.

3. **BAKE** 40 min. or until center is set and top is golden brown.

MAKE AHEAD:
Assemble recipe as directed. Refrigerate up to 24 hours. When ready to serve, uncover and bake as directed.

NUTRITION BONUS:
Wow your guests with this tasty, super simple dish that's packed with nutrition! Not only is the spinach high in vitamin A, but the red bell pepper is a good source of vitamin C and the cheese provides calcium. For complete nutritional information, please visit www.kraftfoods.com.

ham and cheese
stuff'n puff

PREP: 5 min. | TOTAL: 1 hour 10 min. | MAKES: 6 servings.

▶ what you need!

5 eggs

1 cup milk

½ cup BREAKSTONE'S or KNUDSEN Sour Cream

1 pkg. (10 oz.) frozen chopped broccoli, thawed, drained

1 pkg. (6 oz.) STOVE TOP Stuffing Mix for Chicken

1½ pkg. (6 oz. each) OSCAR MAYER Smoked Ham, chopped

1 cup KRAFT Shredded Cheddar Cheese, divided

▶ make it!

HEAT oven to 375°F.

1. **BEAT** eggs, milk and sour cream in large bowl with whisk until well blended. Add broccoli, stuffing mix, ham and ½ cup cheese; mix lightly.

2. **POUR** into 2-qt. casserole; cover loosely with foil.

3. **BAKE** 1 hour. Uncover. Sprinkle with remaining cheese; bake 5 min. or until cheese is melted and broccoli mixture is heated through.

HEALTHY LIVING:
Save 40 calories and 5 grams of fat per serving by preparing with fat-free milk, BREAKSTONE'S Reduced Fat or KNUDSEN Light Sour Cream and KRAFT 2% Milk Shredded Cheddar Cheese.

SUBSTITUTE:
Use whatever frozen vegetables and shredded cheese you have on hand, such as peas and KRAFT Shredded Mozzarella Cheese.

swiss cheese, ham and asparagus bake

PREP: 10 min. | TOTAL: 40 min. | MAKES: 6 servings.

► what you need!

1½ cups hot water

1 pkg. (6 oz.) STOVE TOP Stuffing Mix for Chicken

3 cups cubed cooked ham

½ lb. fresh asparagus, cut into 2-inch lengths

1 can (10¾ oz.) condensed cream of celery soup

½ cup milk

1 cup KRAFT Shredded Swiss Cheese

► make it!

HEAT oven to 350°F.

1. **ADD** hot water to stuffing mix; stir just until moistened. Let stand 5 min.

2. **COMBINE** ham, asparagus, soup and milk in 13×9-inch baking dish; sprinkle with cheese. Top with stuffing.

3. **BAKE** 30 min. or until heated through.

CREATIVE LEFTOVERS:
This is a great way to use leftover baked ham.

STOVE TOP
easy brunch casserole

PREP: 15 min. | TOTAL: 50 min. | MAKES: 8 servings.

▶ what you need!

2 cups STOVE TOP Stuffing Mix for Chicken in the Canister

2 cups milk

1 pkg. (8 oz.) OSCAR MAYER Bacon, cooked, crumbled

6 eggs

1 cup KRAFT Shredded Cheddar Cheese

½ tsp. salt

▶ make it!

HEAT oven to 350°F.

1. **MIX** all ingredients in large bowl.

2. **SPOON** into greased 13×9-inch pan.

3. **BAKE** 45 to 50 min. or until center is set.

SPECIAL EXTRA:
Add 1 cup chopped leftover cooked potatoes to stuffing mixture before spooning into pan.

stuffin' egg muffin

PREP: 10 min. | TOTAL: 30 min. | MAKES: 6 servings.

▸ what you need!

1 pkg. (6 oz.) STOVE TOP Stuffing Mix for Chicken

12 eggs

3 Tbsp. OSCAR MAYER Real Bacon Bits

½ cup KRAFT Shredded Colby & Monterey Jack Cheese

▸ make it!

HEAT oven to 400°F.

1. **PREPARE** stuffing as directed on package, omitting the stand time. Press ¼ cup stuffing onto bottom and up side of each of 12 muffin cups sprayed with cooking spray, forming ¼-inch rim around top of cup.

2. **ADD** 1 egg to each cup. Top with bacon and cheese.

3. **BAKE** 20 min. or until yolks are set. Let stand 5 min. before serving.

SERVING SUGGESTION:
Pack these Stuffin' Egg Muffins with a piece of fruit for a great portable breakfast or lunch.

MAKE AHEAD:
Prepare recipe as directed; cool completely. Refrigerate until ready to serve. To reheat, wrap 2 muffins in waxed paper; microwave on HIGH 15 sec. or just until warmed. Repeat with additional muffins as needed.

vegetable & stuffing bake

PREP: 10 min. | TOTAL: 35 min. | MAKES: 6 servings.

▶ what you need!

¾ cup MIRACLE WHIP Dressing

½ cup milk

1 pkg. (6 oz.) STOVE TOP Stuffing Mix for Chicken

1 pkg. (16 oz.) frozen broccoli florets, thawed, drained

1 cup KRAFT Shredded Cheddar Cheese

▶ make it!

HEAT oven to 350°F.

1. **MIX** dressing and milk in large bowl until blended. Add remaining ingredients; mix lightly.

2. **SPOON** into 8-inch square baking dish.

3. **BAKE** 20 to 25 min. or until heated through.

MAKE AHEAD:
Assemble casserole as directed. Refrigerate up to 24 hours. When ready to serve, uncover and bake at 350°F for 25 to 30 min. or until heated through.

SPECIAL EXTRA:
Add 2 cups chopped turkey or chicken for a heartier dish.

NUTRITION BONUS:
For complete nutritional information, please visit www.kraftfoods.com.

Bakes, Casseroles & Skillets

HEARTY FAMILY FAVORITES

jude's chicken casserole

PREP: 5 min. | TOTAL: 35 min. | MAKES: 6 servings.

▸ what you need!

1 pkg. (6 oz.) STOVE TOP Stuffing Mix for Chicken

2 cups chopped cooked chicken

1 can (10¾ oz.) condensed cream of chicken soup

½ lb. (8 oz.) VELVEETA Pasteurized Prepared Cheese Product, cut into ½-inch cubes

▸ make it!

HEAT oven to 350°F.

1. **PREPARE** stuffing as directed on package. Combine remaining ingredients in large bowl. Add stuffing; mix lightly.

2. **SPOON** into 2-qt. casserole.

3. **BAKE** 30 min. or until heated through.

HEALTHY LIVING:
Good news! You'll save 70 calories and 6 grams of fat, including 3 grams of saturated fat, per serving by preparing with reduced-fat soup and VELVEETA Made With 2% Milk Pasteurized Prepared Cheese Product.

SPECIAL EXTRA:
Prepare as directed, adding ½ cup chopped celery and/or red peppers to chicken mixture before baking.

STOVE TOP
one-dish chicken bake

PREP: 10 min. | TOTAL: 40 min. | MAKES: 6 servings.

► what you need!

1⅔ cups hot water

1 pkg. (6 oz.) STOVE TOP Stuffing Mix for Chicken

1½ lb. boneless skinless chicken breasts, cut into bite-size pieces

1 can (10¾ oz.) condensed cream of mushroom soup

⅓ cup BREAKSTONE'S or KNUDSEN Sour Cream

► make it!

HEAT oven to 400°F.

1. **ADD** hot water to stuffing mix; stir just until moistened.

2. **PLACE** chicken in 13×9-inch baking dish or 2-qt. casserole. Mix soup and sour cream until well blended; pour over chicken. Top with stuffing.

3. **BAKE** 30 min. or until chicken is done.

SERVING SUGGESTION:
Serve with a steamed green vegetable, such as broccoli, and a glass of fat-free milk.

SPECIAL EXTRA:
Prepare as directed, topping chicken with 1 cup frozen mixed vegetables before covering with soup mixture.

STORAGE KNOW-HOW:
Package boneless skinless chicken breast halves in recipe-size portions in the freezer. Thaw only the amount needed for a recipe.

bruschetta chicken bake

PREP: 10 min. | TOTAL: 40 min. | MAKES: 6 servings.

▶ what you need!

   1 can (14½ oz.) diced tomatoes, undrained

   1 pkg. (6 oz.) STOVE TOP Stuffing Mix for Chicken

   ½ cup water

   2 cloves garlic, minced

1½ lb. boneless skinless chicken breasts, cut into bite-size pieces

   1 tsp. dried basil leaves

   1 cup KRAFT 2% Milk Shredded Mozzarella Cheese

▶ make it!

HEAT oven to 400°F.

1. **MIX** tomatoes, stuffing mix, water and garlic just until stuffing mix is moistened.

2. **LAYER** chicken, basil and cheese in 3-qt. casserole or 13×9-inch baking dish.

3. **TOP** with stuffing. Bake 30 min. or until chicken is done.

MAKE AHEAD:
Prepare and bake as directed; cool. Refrigerate up to 24 hours. To reheat, spoon each serving onto microwaveable plate. Microwave on HIGH 2 to 3 min. or until heated through.

NUTRITION BONUS:
Make this flavorful chicken recipe tonight as part of an easy weeknight dinner. As a bonus, the cheese is a good source of calcium. For complete nutritional information, please visit www.kraftfoods.com.

STOVE TOP
easy chicken bake

PREP: 10 min. | TOTAL: 40 min. | MAKES: 6 servings.

▶ what you need!

1 pkg. (6 oz.) STOVE TOP Stuffing Mix for Chicken

1½ lb. boneless skinless chicken breasts, cut into bite-size pieces

1 can (10¾ oz.) condensed cream of chicken soup

⅓ cup BREAKSTONE'S or KNUDSEN Sour Cream

1 pkg. (16 oz.) frozen mixed vegetables, thawed, drained

▶ make it!

HEAT oven to 400°F.

1. **PREPARE** stuffing as directed on package.

2. **MIX** remaining ingredients in 13×9-inch baking dish; top with stuffing.

3. **BAKE** 30 min. or until chicken is done. Enjoy now or cover and refrigerate. To reheat, microwave each serving on HIGH 2 min. or until heated through.

HEALTHY LIVING:
Save 30 calories and 3 grams of fat per serving by preparing with reduced-fat condensed cream of chicken soup and BREAKSTONE'S Reduced Fat or KNUDSEN Light Sour Cream.

STORAGE KNOW-HOW:
Package boneless skinless chicken breasts in recipe-size portions in the freezer. Thaw only the amount needed for a recipe.

STOVE TOP
easy cheesy chicken bake

PREP: 10 min. | TOTAL: 40 min. | MAKES: 6 servings.

▶ what you need!

1 pkg. (6 oz.) STOVE TOP Stuffing Mix for Chicken

1½ lb. boneless skinless chicken breasts, cut into bite-size pieces

1 pkg. (14 oz.) frozen broccoli florets, thawed, drained

1 can (10¾ oz.) condensed cream of chicken soup

½ cup milk

1½ cups KRAFT Shredded Cheddar Cheese

▶ make it!

HEAT oven to 400°F.

1. **PREPARE** stuffing as directed on package.

2. **COMBINE** chicken and broccoli in 13×9-inch baking dish. Stir in soup, milk and cheese; top with stuffing.

3. **BAKE** 30 min. or until chicken is done and casserole is heated through.

SUBSTITUTE:
Prepare using fresh broccoli florets.

cheesy chicken & broccoli bake

PREP: 10 min. | TOTAL: 50 min. | MAKES: 6 servings.

▶ what you need!

1 pkg. (6 oz.) STOVE TOP Stuffing Mix for Chicken

1½ lb. boneless skinless chicken breasts, cut into bite-size pieces

1 pkg. (16 oz.) frozen broccoli florets, thawed, drained

1 can (10¾ oz.) reduced-sodium condensed cream of chicken soup

½ lb. (8 oz.) VELVEETA Pasteurized Prepared Cheese Product, cut into ½-inch cubes

▶ make it!

HEAT oven to 400°F.

1. **PREPARE** stuffing as directed on package; set aside.

2. **COMBINE** remaining ingredients; spoon into 13×9-inch baking dish. Top with stuffing.

3. **BAKE** 40 min. or until chicken is done.

CHICKEN & GREEN BEAN BAKE:
Omit VELVEETA. Prepare as directed, using STOVE TOP Traditional Sage Stuffing Mix and substituting frozen green beans for the broccoli.

easy chicken pot pie

PREP: 10 min. | TOTAL: 40 min. | MAKES: 6 servings.

▸ what you need!

1⅔ cups hot water

1 pkg. (6 oz.) STOVE TOP Lower Sodium Stuffing Mix for Chicken

3 cups chopped cooked chicken

1 pkg. (10 oz.) frozen mixed vegetables

1 can (10¾ oz.) less sodium condensed cream of chicken soup

1 cup milk

▸ make it!

HEAT oven to 375°F.

1. **ADD** hot water to stuffing mix; stir just until moistened.

2. **COMBINE** chicken and vegetables in 2-qt. casserole. Mix soup and milk; pour over chicken mixture. Top with stuffing.

3. **BAKE** 30 min. or until hot and bubbly.

SHORTCUT:
Prepare using 2 pkg. (6 oz. each) OSCAR MAYER Deli Fresh Oven Roasted Chicken Breast Cuts.

SPECIAL EXTRA:
Add ¼ tsp. dried thyme leaves to chicken mixture before topping with soup mixture.

NUTRITION BONUS:
Help your friends and family eat right by serving this low-calorie, low-fat meal. For complete nutritional information, please visit www.kraftfoods.com.

cranberry-orange chicken bake

PREP: 10 min. | TOTAL: 40 min. | MAKES: 6 servings.

▶ what you need!

1 pkg. (6 oz.) STOVE TOP Stuffing Mix for Chicken

1 cup orange juice

½ cup water

⅓ cup dried cranberries

2 Tbsp. chopped PLANTERS Pecans

1½ lb. boneless skinless chicken breasts, cut into bite-size pieces

1 can (10¾ oz.) condensed cream of chicken soup

2 cups frozen mixed vegetables, thawed, drained

▶ make it!

HEAT oven to 400°F.

1. **PREPARE** stuffing as directed on package, using orange juice and water for the liquid and stirring in cranberries and nuts with the stuffing mix.

2. **COMBINE** chicken, soup and vegetables. Spoon into 6 ovenproof serving bowls or 13×9-inch baking dish; top with stuffing mixture.

3. **BAKE** 30 min. or until chicken is done.

SUBSTITUTE:
Substitute boneless skinless chicken thighs for the chicken breasts.

BONUS:
There's no need to skimp on flavor when choosing lean meats to help you eat right. For complete nutritional information, please visit www.kraftfoods.com.

layered meatball bake

PREP: 10 min. | TOTAL: 35 min. | MAKES: 6 servings.

▶ what you need!

1 pkg. (6 oz.) STOVE TOP Stuffing Mix for Chicken

1 can (10¾ oz.) reduced-sodium condensed cream of mushroom soup

¼ cup milk

1 pkg. (1 lb.) frozen meatballs

2 cups frozen peas

1 cup KRAFT 2% Milk Shredded Cheddar Cheese

▶ make it!

HEAT oven to 400°F.

1. **PREPARE** stuffing as directed on package.

2. **MIX** soup and milk in 13×9-inch baking dish. Stir in meatballs and peas; sprinkle with cheese. Top with stuffing.

3. **BAKE** 20 to 25 min. or until heated through.

SERVING SUGGESTION:
Serve this main dish with a mixed green salad for a quick and tasty weekday meal.

VARIATION:
Prepare as directed, substituting 1 can (14½ oz.) diced tomatoes for the soup, omitting milk and using Italian-flavored meatballs and KRAFT Shredded Low-Moisture Part-Skim Mozzarella Cheese.

chili-beef stuffing bake

PREP: 10 min. | TOTAL: 40 min. | MAKES: 6 servings.

▶ what you need!

1½ cups hot water

1 pkg. (6 oz.) STOVE TOP Cornbread Stuffing Mix

1½ lb. lean ground beef

1 can (15 oz.) kidney beans, undrained

1 can (8 oz.) tomato sauce

1 cup TACO BELL® HOME ORIGINALS® Thick 'N Chunky Salsa

1 cup KRAFT Shredded Cheddar Cheese

▶ make it!

HEAT oven to 400°F.

1. **ADD** hot water to stuffing mix; stir just until moistened.

2. **BROWN** meat in large skillet; drain. Stir in beans, tomato sauce and salsa. Spoon into 2-qt. casserole; top with cheese and stuffing.

3. **BAKE** 30 min. or until heated through.

SUBSTITUTE:
Prepare using KRAFT 2% Milk Shredded Cheddar Cheese.

VARIATION:
Omit salsa. Prepare as directed, decreasing oven temperature to 375°F, increasing water to 1⅔ cups and adding 1 Tbsp. chili powder with beans and tomato sauce.

TACO BELL® and HOME ORIGINALS® are trademarks owned and licensed by Taco Bell Corp.

STOVE TOP
easy turkey bake

PREP: 10 min. │ TOTAL: 40 min. │ MAKES: 6 servings.

▶ what you need!

1⅔ cups hot water

1 pkg. (6 oz.) STOVE TOP Stuffing Mix for Turkey

4 cups chopped cooked turkey

1 pkg. (14 oz.) frozen broccoli florets, thawed, drained

1 can (10¾ oz.) condensed cream of chicken soup

¾ cup milk

1½ cups KRAFT Shredded Cheddar Cheese

▶ make it!

HEAT oven to 350°F.

1. **ADD** hot water to stuffing mix; stir just until moistened.

2. **COMBINE** turkey and broccoli in 13×9-inch baking dish. Mix soup, milk and cheese; pour over turkey mixture. Top with stuffing.

3. **BAKE** 30 min. or until heated through.

VARIATION:
Don't have leftover turkey? Prepare recipe as directed, using chopped cooked chicken and STOVE TOP Stuffing Mix for Chicken instead.

STOVE TOP
one-dish chicken skillet

PREP: 5 min. | TOTAL: 25 min. | MAKES: 6 servings.

▶ what you need!

1½ cups hot water

¼ cup (½ stick) butter or margarine, melted

1 pkg. (6 oz.) STOVE TOP Stuffing Mix for Chicken

6 small boneless skinless chicken breast halves (1½ lb.)

1 can (10¾ oz.) condensed cream of mushroom soup

⅓ cup BREAKSTONE'S or KNUDSEN Sour Cream

▶ make it!

1. **MIX** hot water, butter and stuffing mix; set aside.

2. **SPRAY** nonstick skillet with cooking spray. Add chicken; cook on medium heat 5 min. on each side.

3. **MIX** soup and sour cream; pour over chicken. Top with stuffing; cover. Cook on low heat 10 min. or until chicken is done.

SERVING SUGGESTION:
Serve with a bagged salad tossed with your favorite KRAFT Light Dressing.

USE YOUR OVEN:
Heat oven to 375°F. Prepare stuffing as directed. Place chicken in 13×9-inch baking dish or 2-qt. casserole. Mix soup and sour cream; pour over chicken. Top with stuffing. Bake 35 min. or until chicken is done.

french onion-pork chop skillet

PREP: 10 min. | TOTAL: 35 min. | MAKES: 6 servings.

▸ what you need!

6 boneless pork chops (1½ lb.), ½-inch thick

2 onions, thinly sliced

2 Tbsp. Worcestershire sauce

1 pkg. (6 oz.) STOVE TOP Stuffing Mix for Chicken

1½ cups hot water

1 cup KRAFT Shredded Low-Moisture Part-Skim Mozzarella Cheese

▸ make it!

1. **HEAT** large nonstick skillet sprayed with cooking spray on medium-high heat. Add chops and onions; cook 10 min. or until chops are done, turning chops and stirring onions after 5 min. Remove chops from skillet. Cook and stir onions 5 min. or until golden brown.

2. **STIR** in Worcestershire sauce. Return chops to skillet; top with onion mixture.

3. **MIX** stuffing mix and hot water; spoon around edge of skillet. Top with cheese; cover. Cook 5 min. or until cheese is melted.

SERVING SUGGESTION:
Serve with hot steamed broccoli or green beans.

chicken & stuffing florentine

PREP: 10 min. | TOTAL: 40 min. | MAKES: 4 servings.

▶ what you need!

2 cups STOVE TOP Stuffing Mix for Chicken in the Canister

1 cup hot water

¼ cup KRAFT Grated Parmesan Cheese

4 small boneless skinless chicken breast halves (1 lb.)

1 can (10¾ oz.) condensed cream of chicken soup

1 pkg. (10 oz.) frozen chopped spinach, thawed, well drained

▶ make it!

HEAT oven to 400°F.

1. **MIX** stuffing mix, hot water and cheese just until stuffing mix is moistened.

2. **PLACE** chicken in 13×9-inch baking dish. Mix soup and spinach; spoon over chicken. Top with stuffing mixture.

3. **BAKE** 30 min. or until chicken is done.

SUBSTITUTE:
Prepare using 3 cups chopped fresh spinach.

Entrées

EASY AND ELEGANT MAIN MEALS

bruschetta 'n cheese-stuffed chicken breasts

PREP: 15 min. | TOTAL: 1 hour | MAKES: 8 servings.

▶ what you need!

1 can (14½ oz.) Italian-style diced tomatoes, undrained

1¼ cups KRAFT Shredded Low-Moisture Part-Skim Mozzarella Cheese, divided

¼ cup chopped fresh basil

1 pkg. (6 oz.) STOVE TOP Stuffing Mix for Chicken

8 small boneless skinless chicken breast halves (2 lb.)

⅓ cup KRAFT Roasted Red Pepper Italian with Parmesan Dressing

▶ make it!

HEAT oven to 350°F.

1. **MIX** tomatoes, ½ cup cheese and basil in medium bowl. Add stuffing mix; stir just until moistened.

2. **PLACE** 2 chicken breasts in large freezer-weight resealable plastic bag. Pound with meat mallet or side of heavy can until chicken is ¼-inch thick. Remove from bag; place, top-sides down, on cutting board. Repeat with remaining chicken. Spread chicken with stuffing mixture. Starting at 1 narrow end, tightly roll up each breast. Place, seam-sides down, in 13×9-inch baking dish. Drizzle with dressing.

3. **BAKE** 40 min. or until chicken is done. Sprinkle with remaining cheese; bake 5 min. or until melted.

VARIATION:
For a south-of-the-border-style chicken dish, use diced tomatoes with bell or jalapeño peppers, KRAFT Mexican Style Shredded Cheese instead of the mozzarella cheese and chopped cilantro instead of the basil.

easy chicken cordon bleu

PREP: 10 min. | TOTAL: 40 min. | MAKES: 6 servings.

▶ what you need!

1 pkg. (6 oz.) STOVE TOP Lower Sodium Stuffing Mix for Chicken

6 small boneless skinless chicken breast halves (1½ lb.)

6 slices OSCAR MAYER Thin Sliced Smoked Ham

1 can (10¾ oz.) reduced-sodium condensed cream of chicken soup

1 Tbsp. GREY POUPON Dijon Mustard

6 KRAFT DELI FRESH Swiss Cheese Slices

▶ make it!

HEAT oven to 400°F.

1. **PREPARE** stuffing as directed on package.

2. **PLACE** chicken in 13×9-inch baking dish; cover with ham. Mix soup and mustard; spoon over chicken. Top with stuffing.

3. **BAKE** 25 min. or until chicken is done. Top with cheese; bake 5 min. or until melted.

SERVING SUGGESTION:
Serve with hot steamed broccoli for a quick-and-tasty weeknight dinner.

SUBSTITUTE:
Substitute 1½ cups KRAFT Shredded Swiss Cheese or KRAFT Shredded Low-Moisture Part-Skim Mozzarella Cheese for the cheese slices.

creamy broccoli-stuffed chicken breasts

PREP: 15 min. | TOTAL: 45 min. | MAKES: 6 servings.

▶ what you need!

1 pkg. (6 oz.) STOVE TOP Stuffing Mix for Chicken

1 cup water

6 small boneless skinless chicken breast halves (1½ lb.)

1 pkg. (10 oz.) frozen chopped broccoli, thawed, drained

1 can (10¾ oz.) 98% fat-free condensed cream of chicken soup

½ cup fat-free milk

1 tsp. paprika

2 Tbsp. KRAFT Grated Parmesan Cheese

▶ make it!

HEAT oven to 400°F.

1. **COMBINE** stuffing mix and water in large bowl. Let stand 5 min. Meanwhile, pound chicken to ¼-inch thickness. Add broccoli to stuffing; mix lightly. Spread onto chicken to within ½ inch of edges; roll up starting at one short end of each.

2. **PLACE**, seam-sides down, in 13×9-inch baking dish. Mix soup and milk; pour over chicken. Top with paprika and cheese.

3. **BAKE** 30 min. or until chicken is done.

SUBSTITUTE:
Prepare using 98% fat-free condensed cream of mushroom soup.

NUTRITION BONUS:
Enjoy this low-calorie, low-fat entrée made with better-for-you products to help your family eat right. For complete nutritional information, please visit www. kraftfoods.com.

spinach-stuffed chicken breasts

PREP: 25 min. | TOTAL: 1 hour 5 min. | MAKES: 6 servings.

▶ what you need!

1½ cups water

6 Tbsp. KRAFT Roasted Red Pepper Italian with Parmesan Dressing, divided

1 pkg. (10 oz.) spinach leaves, stems removed, chopped

1 pkg. (6 oz.) STOVE TOP Stuffing Mix for Chicken

¼ cup coarsely chopped roasted red peppers

6 small boneless skinless chicken breast halves (1½ lb.), pounded to ¼-inch thickness

½ cup KRAFT Shredded Low-Moisture Part-Skim Mozzarella Cheese

▶ make it!

HEAT oven to 350°F.

1. **BRING** water and 2 Tbsp. dressing to boil in large skillet on medium-high heat. Stir in spinach, stuffing mix and peppers; cover. Remove from heat. Let stand 5 min.

2. **SPREAD** onto chicken breasts. Roll up each breast, starting at 1 short end; place, seam-side down, in 13×9-inch baking dish. Brush with remaining dressing.

3. **BAKE** 35 min. or until chicken is done. Sprinkle with cheese; bake 5 min. or until melted.

NUTRITION BONUS:
Enjoy this elegant and tasty main dish as part of your overall healthful eating plan. As a bonus, the spinach provides an excellent source of vitamin A! For complete nutritional information, please visit www.kraftfoods.com.

foil-pack chicken & mushroom dinner

PREP: 10 min. | TOTAL: 45 min. | MAKES: 6 servings.

▶ what you need!

1 can (10¾ oz.) condensed cream of mushroom soup

1¼ cups water, divided

1 pkg. (6 oz.) STOVE TOP Stuffing Mix for Chicken

6 small boneless skinless chicken breast halves (1½ lb.), ½-inch thick

4 slices OSCAR MAYER Thin Sliced Smoked Ham, chopped

1½ cups sliced fresh mushrooms

1½ cups frozen peas

▶ make it!

HEAT oven to 400°F.

1.

2.

3.

MIX soup and ¼ cup water. Combine stuffing mix and remaining water; spoon onto centers of 6 large sheets of heavy-duty foil.

TOP with chicken, ham, vegetables and soup mixture.

BRING up foil sides. Double fold top and both ends to seal each packet, leaving room for heat circulation inside. Place in 5×10×1-inch pan. Bake 30 to 35 min. or until chicken is done. Remove packets from oven; let stand 5 min.

CUT slits in tops of packets to release steam before opening.

COOKING KNOW-HOW:
To prevent stuffing from sticking to foil, spray foil with cooking spray before using, or use nonstick foil.

COOKING KNOW-HOW:
If the chicken breast halves in your market are larger than ¼ lb. each, they will take longer to cook. Be sure to cook them long enough so that they are no longer pink in the centers and the juices run clear.

STOVE TOP
sweet citrus chicken

PREP: 10 min. | TOTAL: 40 min. | MAKES: 6 servings.

▶ what you need!

1⅔ cups hot water

1 pkg. (6 oz.) STOVE TOP Stuffing Mix for Chicken

6 small boneless skinless chicken breast halves (1½ lb.), pounded to ½-inch thickness

⅔ cup orange juice

⅓ cup packed brown sugar

3 Tbsp. butter or margarine, melted

▶ make it!

HEAT oven to 400°F.

1. **ADD** hot water to stuffing mix; stir just until moistened.

2. **PLACE** chicken in 13×9-inch baking dish. Mix juice, sugar and butter until blended; pour over chicken. Top with stuffing.

3. **BAKE** 30 min. or until chicken is done.

SUBSTITUTE:
Substitute honey for the brown sugar.

easy cheesy
stuffed chicken

PREP: 30 min. | TOTAL: 1 hour 25 min. | MAKES: 8 servings.

▶ what you need!

2 Tbsp. butter or margarine

2 zucchini, shredded (about 2 cups)

1 onion, chopped

1 pkg. (6 oz.) STOVE TOP Stuffing Mix for Chicken

1 cup KRAFT Finely Shredded Italian Five Cheese Blend

2 chickens (5 lb.), quartered

¾ cup KRAFT Honey Barbecue Sauce

▶ make it!

HEAT oven to 400°F.

1. **MELT** butter in medium saucepan on medium heat. Add zucchini and onions; cook and stir 2 min. or until tender. Remove from heat. Stir in stuffing mix and cheese until well blended.

2. **INSERT** fingers carefully between the meat and skin of each chicken quarter to form a pocket. Fill pockets with stuffing mixture. Place, skin-sides up, in large roasting pan.

3. **BAKE** 45 min. or until chicken is done. Brush with barbecue sauce. Bake 5 to 10 min. or until heated through.

SIZE-WISE:
Serve this simple main dish for your friends and family at your next winter dinner party.

SUBSTITUTE:
This recipe can easily be turned into a Mexican-style chicken dish by preparing with KRAFT Mexican Style Finely Shredded Four Cheese.

super crunch chicken

PREP: 10 min. | TOTAL: 40 min. | MAKES: 4 servings.

▶ what you need!

8 boneless skinless chicken thighs (1 lb.)

¼ cup MIRACLE WHIP Light Dressing

1 pkg. (6 oz.) STOVE TOP Stuffing Mix for Chicken

¼ cup KRAFT Grated Parmesan Cheese

▶ make it!

HEAT oven to 375°F.

1. **SPREAD** chicken with dressing.

2. **MIX** stuffing mix and cheese in pie plate. Add chicken, 1 piece at a time; turn to evenly coat. Place on foil-covered baking sheet. Discard any leftover stuffing mixture.

3. **BAKE** 25 to 30 min. or until chicken is done.

SERVING SUGGESTION:
Serve with fresh vegetable sticks, such as carrots, celery and cucumbers, and a fresh fruit salad.

pork chops with apples and stuffing

PREP: 10 min. | TOTAL: 50 min. | MAKES: 6 servings.

▸ what you need!

1 pkg. (6 oz.) STOVE TOP Stuffing Mix for Chicken

1 can (21 oz.) apple pie filling

6 boneless pork loin chops (1½ lb.), ¾-inch thick

▸ make it!

HEAT oven to 375°F.

1. **PREPARE** stuffing as directed on package.

2. **SPREAD** pie filling onto bottom of 13×9-inch baking dish sprayed with cooking spray; top with chops and stuffing. Cover with foil.

3. **BAKE** 40 min. or until chops are done, removing foil after 30 min.

SUBSTITUTE:
Prepare using 6 boneless skinless chicken breast halves.

SPECIAL EXTRA:
Certain flavors go extremely well with pork. So if you want to pair pork chops or a roast with the perfect ingredients, try these suggestions: Thyme, sage, bay leaves, garlic, mustard, apples, prunes, pineapple and sauerkraut.

harvest stuffed pork loin

PREP: 15 min. │ TOTAL: 1 hour │ MAKES: 16 servings.

▶ what you need!

1 pkg. (6 oz.) STOVE TOP Stuffing Mix for Chicken

2 apples, peeled, chopped

3 Tbsp. dried cranberries

1 cup chopped toasted PLANTERS Pecans

1 Tbsp. dried sage leaves

1 center-cut pork loin (4 lb.), butterflied

½ tsp. salt

½ tsp. black pepper

▶ make it!

HEAT oven to 400°F.

1. **PREPARE** stuffing as directed on package. Remove from heat; gently stir in fruit, nuts and sage.

2. **UNROLL** meat; spread with stuffing mixture. Roll up, starting at one long side. Place, seam-side down, on foil-covered baking sheet sprayed with cooking spray. Season with salt and pepper.

3. **BAKE** 45 min. or until meat is done. Let stand 10 min. before slicing.

SERVING SUGGESTION:
Serve with hot steamed vegetables, such as carrots and broccoli.

SUBSTITUTE:
Prepare using 3 Tbsp. chopped fresh sage.

pork medallions with cranberry stuffing

PREP: 5 min. | TOTAL: 20 min. | MAKES: 6 servings.

▶ what you need!

 2 pork tenderloins (1½ lb.)

 ¼ cup KRAFT Sun-Dried Tomato Dressing

 1 Tbsp. GREY POUPON Dijon Mustard

 1 pkg. (6 oz.) STOVE TOP Stuffing Mix for Chicken

 ⅓ cup dried cranberries

▶ make it!

1. **CUT** each tenderloin crosswise into 6 slices; pound to ½-inch thickness. Cook in large nonstick skillet sprayed with cooking spray on medium-high heat 3 min. on each side or until browned on both sides.

2. **MIX** dressing and mustard; pour over meat. Cook on low heat 3 min. on each side or until meat is done and sauce is thickened. Meanwhile, prepare stuffing as directed on package, but reducing spread to 1 Tbsp. and adding cranberries to water along with stuffing mix.

3. **SPOON** stuffing onto serving plates. Add meat; top with sauce.

SERVING SUGGESTION:
Serve with a crisp mixed green salad tossed with your favorite KRAFT Light Dressing.

NUTRITION BONUS:
Good news! This oh-so-easy combination has foods from two different food groups, helping you to eat a variety of foods. For complete nutritional information, please visit www.kraftfoods.com.

peach-glazed pork chops

PREP: 15 min. | TOTAL: 55 min. | MAKES: 6 servings.

▶ what you need!

1 can (8½ oz.) peach slices in juice, undrained

Hot water

¼ cup (½ stick) butter or margarine, cut up

1 pkg. (6 oz.) STOVE TOP Stuffing Mix for Pork

6 bone-in pork chops (1½ lb.), ½-inch thick

⅓ cup peach or apricot preserves

1 Tbsp. GREY POUPON Savory Honey Mustard

▶ make it!

HEAT oven to 375°F.

1. **DRAIN** peaches, reserving juice. Add enough hot water to reserved juice to make 1½ cups; pour into large bowl. Add butter; stir until melted. Stir in stuffing mix and peaches. Let stand 5 min.

2. **SPOON** into 13×9-inch pan; top with chops. Mix preserves and mustard; spoon over chops.

3. **BAKE** 40 min. or until chops are done.

SUBSTITUTE:
Prepare using STOVE TOP Stuffing Mix for Chicken.

jumbo meatballs

PREP: 10 min. | TOTAL: 40 min. | MAKES: 4 servings.

▶ what you need!

1 pkg. (6 oz.) STOVE TOP Stuffing Mix for Chicken

½ cup hot water

1 egg

¼ cup KRAFT Ranch Dressing

1 lb. lean ground beef

1 cup KRAFT Shredded Cheddar Cheese

⅓ cup ketchup

▶ make it!

HEAT oven to 375°F.

1. **COMBINE** first 4 ingredients in large bowl. Add meat and cheese; mix well. Shape into 8 (2-inch) meatballs.

2. **PLACE** on greased baking sheet; spread with ketchup.

3. **BAKE** 30 min. or until done.

SERVING SUGGESTION:
Serve with hot cooked rice and steamed broccoli.

easy pleasing meatloaf

PREP: 10 min. | TOTAL: 1 hour 10 min. | MAKES: 8 servings.

► what you need!

2 lb. lean ground beef

1 pkg. (6 oz.) STOVE TOP Stuffing Mix for Chicken

1 cup water

2 eggs, beaten

½ cup KRAFT Original Barbecue Sauce, divided

► make it!

HEAT oven to 375°F.

1.

PLACE meat, stuffing mix, water, eggs and ¼ cup barbecue sauce in bowl.

MIX just until blended.

2.

SHAPE into loaf in 13×9-inch baking dish.

3.

TOP with remaining barbecue sauce. Bake 1 hour or until done.

TO DOUBLE:
Mix meat mixture as directed, doubling all ingredients. Shape into 2 loaves. Place, side-by-side, in 13×9-inch baking dish. Bake at 375°F for 1 hour and 25 min. or until done. Refrigerate leftover meatloaf; use to make sandwiches.

SERVING SUGGESTION:
Serve this comfort food with mashed potatoes and a hot steamed vegetable, such as broccoli.

dressed-up fish
rolls for a crowd

PREP: 10 min. | TOTAL: 35 min. | MAKES: 10 servings.

▸ what you need!

1 pkg. (6 oz.) STOVE TOP Cornbread Stuffing Mix

¾ cup KRAFT Zesty Italian Dressing

¼ cup chopped fresh parsley

½ tsp. garlic powder

¼ tsp. paprika

10 whitefish filets (2½ lb.)

▸ make it!

HEAT oven to 425°F.

1. **PREPARE** stuffing as directed on package; set aside. Mix dressing, parsley and seasonings until well blended; brush half onto fish.

2. **SPOON** stuffing onto 1 end of each fish filet; roll up. Place, seam-sides down, in 13×9-inch baking dish sprayed with cooking spray. Pour remaining dressing mixture over fish.

3. **BAKE** 20 to 25 min. or until fish flakes easily with fork.

COOKING KNOW-HOW:
For best results, use thin flounder or sole filets.

HEALTHY LIVING:
Looking to reduce fat in your diet? Save 3 grams of fat per serving by preparing with KRAFT Light Zesty Italian Dressing. You will save 40 calories per serving, too!

quick & easy crab cakes

PREP: 10 min. | TOTAL: 20 min. | MAKES: 6 servings.

► what you need!

1 cup boiling water

1 pkg. (6 oz.) STOVE TOP Cornbread Stuffing Mix

3 eggs

2 cans (6 oz. each) crabmeat, drained, flaked

¼ cup (½ stick) butter or margarine

1 lemon, cut into 6 wedges

► make it!

1. **ADD** boiling water to stuffing mix; stir just until moistened. Let stand 5 min.

2. **BEAT** eggs in large bowl. Add crabmeat; mix lightly. Stir in stuffing. Shape into 6 patties.

3. **MELT** butter in large skillet on medium heat. Add patties; cook 5 min. on each side or until heated through and lightly browned on both sides. Serve with lemon wedges.

SERVING SUGGESTION:
Serve with small hot baked potatoes and a bagged salad tossed with your favorite KRAFT Dressing, such as Italian.

SPECIAL EXTRA:
Add ¼ cup chopped red peppers and 2 Tbsp. chopped onions to the crabmeat mixture before shaping into patties.

PREP: 10 min. | TOTAL: 35 min. | MAKES: 6 servings.

▶ what you need!

1½ lb. extra lean ground beef

1 pkg. (6 oz.) STOVE TOP Stuffing Mix for Chicken

1½ cups water, divided

¾ cup chopped onions

1 pkg. (8 oz.) fresh mushrooms, sliced

½ cup KRAFT Original Barbecue Sauce

▶ make it!

HEAT oven to 375°F.

1. **MIX** meat, stuffing mix, 1¼ cups water and onions until well blended. Shape into 6 (½-inch-thick) oval patties. Place on 15×10×1-inch pan.

2. **BAKE** 25 min. or until patties are done.

3. **MEANWHILE**, spray large nonstick skillet with cooking spray. Add mushrooms; cook on medium-high heat 5 min. or until lightly browned, stirring occasionally. Add barbecue sauce and remaining water; simmer on low heat 1 to 2 min. or until sauce is heated through. Serve over meat patties.

MAKEOVER - HOW WE DID IT:
We have taken a classic comfort food and made it over by preparing it with extra lean ground beef and cooking the mushrooms in a nonstick skillet instead of in a regular skillet with butter. These changes will save you 15 grams of fat per serving.

SUBSTITUTE:
Prepare using KRAFT Hickory Smoke Barbecue Sauce.

NUTRITION BONUS:
Feel good about serving your friends and family this reduced-fat version of a classic recipe. For complete nutritional information, please visit www.kraftfoods.com.

stuffing-topped beef filets

PREP: 10 min. | TOTAL: 27 min. | MAKES: 2 servings.

▸ what you need!

2 beef tenderloin filets (½ lb.)

1 Tbsp. butter

½ cup shredded zucchini

⅓ cup finely chopped onions

¾ cup STOVE TOP Stuffing Mix for Chicken in the Canister

½ cup KRAFT Shredded Cheddar Cheese

▸ make it!

HEAT broiler.

1. **HEAT** ovenproof skillet on medium heat. Add meat; cook 6 min. on each side or until medium doneness. Remove from skillet; cover to keep warm.

2. **MELT** butter in same skillet on medium-high heat. Add zucchini and onions; cook and stir 2 min. or until crisp-tender. Transfer to large bowl; stir in stuffing mix and cheese. Add meat to skillet; top with stuffing mixture.

3. **BROIL**, 6 inches from heat source, 5 min. or until stuffing is lightly browned.

SERVING SUGGESTION:
Serve with a crisp mixed green salad tossed with your favorite KRAFT Light Dressing.

SUBSTITUTE:
If you are a blue cheese lover, substitute ¼ cup ATHENOS Crumbled Blue Cheese for the ½ cup Cheddar.

Sandwiches
& Sides

SIMPLE DISHES THAT ARE READY IN A SNAP

creamy vegetable bake

PREP: 20 min. | TOTAL: 50 min. | MAKES: 10 servings.

▶ what you need!

1 pkg. (8 oz.) PHILADELPHIA Cream Cheese, softened

⅓ cup milk

¼ cup KRAFT Grated Parmesan Cheese

1 tsp. dried basil leaves

4 large carrots, diagonally sliced

½ lb. sugar snap peas

½ lb. fresh asparagus, cut into 1-inch lengths

1 large red bell pepper, chopped

1 pkg. (6 oz.) STOVE TOP Stuffing Mix for Chicken

▶ make it!

HEAT oven to 350°F.

1. **MICROWAVE** cream cheese and milk in large microwaveable bowl on HIGH 1 min. or until cream cheese is melted and mixture is blended when stirred. Add Parmesan and basil; stir until blended. Add vegetables; toss to coat.

2. **SPOON** into greased 13×9-inch baking dish. Prepare stuffing as directed on package; spoon over vegetable mixture.

3. **BAKE** 30 min. or until golden brown.

SUBSTITUTE:
Prepare using PHILADELPHIA Neufchâtel Cheese.

cheesy green bean casserole

PREP: 10 min. | TOTAL: 40 min. | MAKES: 14 servings.

▸ what you need!

2 bags (16 oz. each) frozen French cut green beans, thawed

1 can (10¾ oz.) condensed cream of mushroom soup

1 cup CHEEZ WHIZ Cheese Dip

1½ cups hot water

¼ cup (½ stick) margarine

1 pkg. (6 oz.) STOVE TOP Stuffing Mix for Chicken

▸ make it!

HEAT oven to 350°F.

1. **COMBINE** beans, soup and CHEEZ WHIZ in 2-qt. casserole.

2. **ADD** hot water to margarine in medium bowl; stir until melted. Stir in stuffing mix just until moistened. Spoon over bean mixture.

3. **BAKE** 30 min. or until heated through.

MAKE AHEAD:
Assemble casserole as directed. Refrigerate up to 24 hours. When ready to serve, bake, uncovered, at 350°F for 45 to 50 min. or until heated through.

broccoli polonaise

PREP: 15 min. | TOTAL: 15 min. | MAKES: 4 servings.

▶ what you need!

1 bunch broccoli, cut into florets (about 4 cups)

1 cup STOVE TOP Stuffing Mix for Chicken in the Canister

2 hard-cooked eggs, chopped

¼ cup (½ stick) butter or margarine, melted

¼ cup KRAFT Grated Parmesan Cheese

▶ make it!

1. **COOK** broccoli in boiling water 5 to 10 min. or until crisp-tender.

2. **MEANWHILE**, mix remaining ingredients.

3. **DRAIN** broccoli; spoon into serving dish. Top with stuffing mixture; cover. Let stand 5 min.

SERVING SUGGESTION:
Enjoy a serving of this vegetable dish at your next get-together along with a serving of your favorite grilled lean meat.

MAKE AHEAD:
Cook broccoli as directed; spoon into casserole. Mix stuffing mix, eggs, butter and cheese; spoon over broccoli. Refrigerate. When ready to serve, bake, uncovered, at 350°F for 10 min. or until heated through.

italian bread
salad with olives

PREP: 20 min. | TOTAL: 1 hour 20 min. (incl. refrigerating) | MAKES: 12 servings.

▶ what you need!

1 cup hot water

4 cups STOVE TOP Stuffing Mix for Chicken in the Canister

1 tomato, seeded, chopped

1 cup chopped red onions

1 cup sliced stuffed green olives

½ cup KRAFT Grated Parmesan Cheese

¾ cup prepared GOOD SEASONS Italian Dressing Mix

▶ make it!

1. **ADD** hot water to stuffing mix in large bowl; stir just until moistened. Cover; let stand 5 min.

2. **STIR** in remaining ingredients.

3. **REFRIGERATE** 1 hour.

BEST OF SEASON:
Use the freshest tomatoes and onions available from your garden or a farmer's market!

SUBSTITUTE:
Prepare using GOOD SEASONS Basil Vinaigrette Dressing Mix.

cheesy broccoli casserole

PREP: 10 min. | TOTAL: 40 min. | MAKES: 8 servings.

▶ what you need!

1 pkg. (6 oz.) STOVE TOP Stuffing Mix for Chicken

2 pkg. (10 oz. each) frozen broccoli florets, thawed, drained

1 can (10¾ oz.) condensed cream of mushroom soup

1 cup CHEEZ WHIZ Cheese Dip

▶ make it!

HEAT oven to 350°F.

1. **PREPARE** stuffing as directed on package, using only 3 Tbsp. margarine.

2. **MIX** remaining ingredients in 2-qt. baking dish; top with stuffing.

3. **BAKE** 30 min. or until heated through.

MAKE AHEAD:
Assemble casserole as directed. Refrigerate up to 24 hours. When ready to serve, bake, uncovered, at 350°F for 45 to 50 min. or until heated through.

easy layered vegetable bake

PREP: 10 min. | TOTAL: 50 min. | MAKES: 6 servings.

▸ what you need!

1 pkg. (6 oz.) STOVE TOP Stuffing Mix for Chicken

5 eggs, divided

1½ cups KRAFT Shredded Cheddar & Monterey Jack Cheese, divided

1 onion, chopped

1 pkg. (10 oz.) frozen chopped spinach, thawed, drained

½ cup red bell pepper strips

2 tomatoes, sliced

▸ make it!

HEAT oven to 400°F.

1. **PREPARE** stuffing as directed on package. Add 1 egg; mix well. Press onto bottom of greased 9-inch square baking dish; sprinkle with ¾ cup cheese.

2. **COOK** and stir onions in medium nonstick skillet sprayed with cooking spray 5 min. or until tender. Remove from heat; stir in spinach. Spoon half over cheese layer in baking dish; top with peppers. Cover with layers of remaining cheese and spinach mixture. Beat remaining eggs; pour over ingredients in baking dish. Top with tomatoes.

3. **BAKE** 35 to 40 min. or until center is set.

COOKING KNOW-HOW:
Cool 5 to 10 min. before cutting into squares to serve.

NOTE:
Refrigerate any leftovers. No need to reheat before serving the next day along with a tossed green salad.

pecan-stuffed squash

PREP: 20 min. | TOTAL: 1 hour 20 min. | MAKES: 6 servings.

▶ what you need!

3 small acorn squash, halved, seeded

1 pkg. (6 oz.) STOVE TOP Stuffing Mix for Chicken

½ cup chopped PLANTERS Pecans

⅓ cup raisins

3 Tbsp. butter, melted

2 Tbsp. brown sugar

▶ make it!

HEAT oven to 350°F.

1. **PLACE** squash, cut-sides down, in foil-lined 15×10×1-inch pan; cover. Bake 30 min.

2. **MEANWHILE**, prepare stuffing as directed on package, decreasing butter to 3 Tbsp. Add nuts and raisins; mix lightly. Turn squash over; spoon stuffing mixture into squash halves.

3. **MIX** butter and sugar; drizzle over squash. Cover. Bake 30 min. or until squash is tender, removing foil after 20 min.

SERVING SUGGESTION:
Serve this autumn side dish with your favorite lean meat and a crisp mixed green salad.

BEST OF SEASON:
Acorn squash is a winter squash which should be relatively heavy with a tough rind.

the ultimate leftover turkey sandwich

PREP: 5 min. | TOTAL: 5 min. | MAKES: 1 serving.

▶ what you need!

2 slices multi-grain bread

1 Tbsp. MIRACLE WHIP Dressing

3 oz. oven-roasted turkey breast, sliced

½ cup prepared STOVE TOP Stuffing Mix for Turkey

2 Tbsp. cranberry sauce

▶ make it!

1. **SPREAD** 1 bread slice with dressing.

2. **TOP** with turkey, stuffing and cranberry sauce.

3. **COVER** with remaining bread slice.

SERVING SUGGESTION:
Serve with a mixed green salad tossed with your favorite KRAFT Dressing.

SPECIAL EXTRA:
For an extra creamy treat, spread second bread slice with 1 Tbsp.
PHILADELPHIA Cream Cheese Spread before adding to sandwich.

savory corn spoon bread

PREP: 10 min. | TOTAL: 55 min. | MAKES: 8 servings.

▶ what you need!

2 cups hot milk

3 Tbsp. butter or margarine, cut into pieces

2 cups STOVE TOP Cornbread Stuffing Mix in the Canister

1 cup frozen corn, thawed

2 eggs, beaten

1 green onion, chopped

2 tsp. sugar

▶ make it!

HEAT oven to 350°F.

1. **ADD** milk to butter in 1½-qt. casserole; stir until butter is melted.

2. **STIR** in remaining ingredients.

3. **BAKE** 45 min. or until knife inserted in center comes out clean.

SPECIAL EXTRA:
Add ¼ cup OSCAR MAYER Real Bacon Bits with stuffing mix.

HOW TO LIGHTLY BEAT EGGS:
For lightly beaten eggs, use a wire whisk or fork to break up yolks and barely combine yolks and whites. For well beaten eggs, mix vigorously to combine yolks and whites until mixture is light and frothy.

meatball sub sandwiches

PREP: 10 min. | TOTAL: 33 min. | MAKES: 4 servings.

▶ what you need!

¼ cup water

½ cup STOVE TOP Stuffing Mix for Chicken in the Canister

1 lb. ground beef

1 egg, beaten

¼ cup KRAFT Grated Parmesan Cheese

4 unsplit Italian bread rolls (7 inch)

1 cup spaghetti sauce

½ cup KRAFT Shredded Mozzarella Cheese

▶ make it!

HEAT oven to 375°F.

1. **ADD** water to stuffing mix in medium bowl; stir just until moistened. Let stand 5 min. Add meat, egg and Parmesan; mix lightly. Shape into 12 (2-inch) meatballs. Place in 15×10×1-inch pan.

2. **BAKE** 15 to 20 min. or until done. Meanwhile, cut thin slice off top of each roll; set aside. Remove bread from insides of rolls, leaving ¼-inch-thick shells. Reserve removed bread for another use.

3. **FILL** each roll with 2 Tbsp. sauce and 3 meatballs; drizzle with additional 2 Tbsp. sauce. Sprinkle with mozzarella. Replace tops of rolls. Bake 2 to 3 min. or until mozzarella is melted.

MAKE AHEAD:
Bake meatballs as directed; cool completely. Place in large resealable freezer-weight plastic bags. Freeze up to 2 months. Remove from freezer and thaw as needed. Warm in the microwave before using to make sandwiches as directed.

smothered chicken sandwich

PREP: 20 min. | TOTAL: 20 min. | MAKES: 6 servings.

▶ what you need!

6 small boneless skinless chicken breast halves (1½ lb.)

1 can (10½ oz.) chicken gravy

1 pkg. (6 oz.) STOVE TOP Stuffing Mix for Chicken

1½ cups hot water

6 slices white bread

3 cups frozen peas, cooked

▶ make it!

1. **COOK** chicken in large nonstick skillet sprayed with cooking spray 3 min. on each side. Add gravy; cook 5 min. or until chicken is done. Meanwhile, mix stuffing mix and hot water.

2. **SPOON** stuffing over chicken; cover. Cook 5 min. or until stuffing is heated through.

3. **TOP** bread with chicken and gravy. Serve with peas.

VARIATION:
Cut each cooked chicken breast horizontally in half before placing on bread slices.

NOTE:
Ingredients can easily be cut in half for a 3-serving version of this tasty recipe.

ham 'n stuff wrap

PREP: 10 min. | TOTAL: 11 min. | MAKES: 1 serving.

► what you need!

- 1   flour tortilla (10 inch)
- 1   Tbsp. MIRACLE WHIP Dressing
- 1   Tbsp. GREY POUPON Dijon Mustard
- ½   cup chopped leftover cooked ham
- ⅓   cup prepared STOVE TOP Stuffing Mix for Chicken
- ¼   cup chopped tomatoes

► make it!

1. **SPREAD** tortilla with dressing and mustard; top with remaining ingredients.

2. **FOLD** in opposite sides of tortilla, then roll up from one end, leaving top end open. Place on microwaveable plate.

3. **MICROWAVE** on HIGH 1 min. or until heated through.

SUBSTITUTE:
Substitute MIRACLE WHIP Light Dressing, KRAFT Real Mayo Mayonnaise or KRAFT Light Mayo Reduced Fat Mayonnaise for the regular MIRACLE WHIP Dressing.

Outside the Box

**NEW AND INNOVATIVE WAYS TO
BRING STUFFING TO THE TABLE**

spinach-stuffed mushrooms

PREP: 15 min. | TOTAL: 35 min. | MAKES: 40 servings.

▶ what you need!

1 pkg. (6 oz.) STOVE TOP Stuffing Mix for Chicken

1½ cups hot water

40 fresh mushrooms (about 2 lb.)

2 Tbsp. butter

2 cloves garlic, minced

1 pkg. (10 oz.) frozen chopped spinach, thawed, well drained

1 cup KRAFT Shredded Low-Moisture Part-Skim Mozzarella Cheese

1 cup KRAFT Grated Parmesan Cheese

▶ make it!

HEAT oven to 400°F.

1. **MIX** stuffing mix and hot water in large bowl; set aside. Remove stems from mushrooms; chop stems. Melt butter in skillet on medium heat. Add chopped stems and garlic; cook and stir until tender. Add to prepared stuffing with spinach and cheeses; mix well.

2. **SPOON** into mushroom caps. Place, filled-sides up, in shallow pan.

3. **BAKE** 20 min. or until mushrooms are tender and filling is heated through.

NUTRITION BONUS:
These appetizers can help you eat right. And as a bonus, they contain spinach which provides vitamin A. For complete nutritional information, please visit www.kraftfoods.com.

stuffing balls

PREP: 15 min. | TOTAL: 35 min. | MAKES: 8 servings.

▸ what you need!

1 lb. ground pork

1 pkg. (6 oz.) STOVE TOP Stuffing Mix for Chicken

¾ cup cranberry sauce

1 egg

1 cup water

2 Tbsp. butter, melted

▸ make it!

HEAT oven to 325°F.

1. **COOK** meat in large skillet until cooked through, stirring frequently; drain. Place in large bowl; cool slightly. Stir in stuffing mix.

2. **ADD** cranberry sauce, egg and water; mix well. Shape into 16 balls; place on foil-covered baking sheet. Brush with butter.

3. **BAKE** 20 min. or until done.

SIZE-WISE:
Enjoy your favorite foods while keeping portion size in mind.

MAKE AHEAD:
Prepare and shape stuffing balls as directed. Freeze in airtight container up to 1 month. Thaw in refrigerator, then bake as directed.

cheesy stuffing cups

PREP: 15 min. | TOTAL: 25 min. | MAKES: 8 servings.

▶ what you need!

¼ cup (½ stick) butter

¾ cup chopped celery

1½ cups water

1 pkg. (6 oz.) STOVE TOP Stuffing Mix for Chicken

⅓ cup dried cranberries

¼ cup coarsely chopped PLANTERS Walnuts

1½ cups KRAFT Shredded Cheddar Cheese, divided

1 egg, beaten

▶ make it!

HEAT oven to 350°F.

1. **MELT** butter in large skillet on medium heat. Add celery; cook and stir 5 min. or until crisp-tender. Stir in water. Bring to boil. Remove from heat. Stir in stuffing mix, cranberries and nuts. Add 1 cup cheese and egg; mix lightly.

2. **SPOON** into 8 greased muffin cups, mounding mixture as necessary to use all the stuffing mixture. Sprinkle with remaining cheese.

3. **BAKE** 10 min. or until stuffing cups are heated through and cheese is melted.

VARIATION:
Don't have a muffin pan? Spoon stuffing mixture into 8 muffin pan liners instead. Place on baking sheet and bake as directed.

STOVE TOP
stuffed shrimp

PREP: 20 min. | TOTAL: 25 min. | MAKES: 8 servings.

▸ what you need!

2 lb. uncooked deveined peeled jumbo shrimp (about 24)

2 Tbsp. olive oil

1 pkg. (6 oz.) STOVE TOP Stuffing Mix for Chicken

▸ make it!

HEAT oven to 400°F.

1. **CUT** slit in underside of each shrimp. Heat oil in large skillet on medium heat. Add shrimp; cook and stir 5 min. or until shrimp turn pink. Place, slit-sides down, in shallow baking dish.

2. **PREPARE** stuffing as directed on package; spoon onto shrimp.

3. **BAKE** 5 min. or until heated through.

FOOD FACTS:
The size of a shrimp is indicated by the number per pound, with the smaller number being the larger shrimp. Jumbo shrimp yield less than 15 shrimp per pound.

STOVE TOP spinach balls

PREP: 15 min. | TOTAL: 35 min. | MAKES: 20 servings.

▶ what you need!

1 pkg. (6 oz.) STOVE TOP Savory Herbs Stuffing Mix

1⅔ cups hot water

¼ cup (½ stick) butter or margarine

2 pkg. (10 oz. each) frozen chopped spinach, thawed, well drained and patted dry

1 cup KRAFT Grated Parmesan Cheese

1 cup chopped fresh mushrooms

1 small onion, finely chopped

4 eggs

▶ make it!

HEAT oven to 400°F.

1. **MIX** stuffing mix, hot water and butter in large bowl until well blended.

2. **ADD** remaining ingredients; mix lightly. Shape into 60 (1-inch) balls. Place in single layer in 2 (15×10×1-inch) pans sprayed with cooking spray.

3. **BAKE** 15 to 20 min. or until lightly browned.

MAKE AHEAD:
Prepare and bake spinach balls as directed; cool completely. Place in freezer-weight resealable plastic bags; freeze up to 3 months. When ready to serve, thaw in refrigerator. Place on baking sheets and bake at 400°F for 10 to 15 min. or until heated through.

 NUTRITION BONUS:
Since these tasty appetizers are rich in vitamin A from the spinach, they can fit into a healthful eating plan. For complete nutritional information, please visit www.kraftfoods.com.

baked italian-style meatballs

PREP: 10 min. | TOTAL: 30 min. | MAKES: 8 servings.

▶ what you need!

2	lb. ground beef
1	pkg. (6 oz.) STOVE TOP Stuffing Mix for Chicken
1¼	cups water
2	eggs, beaten
2	cloves garlic, minced
⅓	cup KRAFT Grated Parmesan Cheese
4	cups small shaped pasta, uncooked
1	cup spaghetti sauce

▶ make it!

HEAT oven to 400°F.

1. **MIX** first 6 ingredients until well blended. Shape into 24 meatballs, using about ¼ cup for each. Place in foil-lined 15×10×1-inch pan.

2. **BAKE** 20 min. or until done. Meanwhile, cook pasta as directed on package and heat spaghetti sauce.

3. **DRAIN** pasta. Serve topped with sauce and meatballs.

HEALTHY LIVING:
Save 60 calories and 8 grams of fat per serving by preparing with extra lean ground beef and substituting ¼ cup cholesterol-free egg product for the eggs.

SERVING SUGGESTION:
Serve with a bagged salad tossed with your favorite KRAFT Light Dressing, such as Zesty Italian.

STOVE TOP
stuffed tomatoes

PREP: 10 min. | TOTAL: 30 min. | MAKES: 6 servings.

▸ what you need!

6 tomatoes

1 cup hot water

¼ cup (½ stick) spread or margarine, cut up

1 pkg. (6 oz.) STOVE TOP Savory Herbs Stuffing Mix

▸ make it!

HEAT oven to 400°F.

1. **CUT** tops off tomatoes; remove seeds and pulp, leaving ¼-inch-thick shells. Chop pulp; drain. Set aside for later use. Discard tomato tops and seeds. Invert shells on paper towels to drain.

2. **MEANWHILE**, combine hot water and spread in large bowl. Stir in stuffing mix and reserved pulp. Let stand 5 min. Place tomato shells in greased shallow baking dish; fill with stuffing mixture.

3. **BAKE** 20 min. or until tomatoes are tender and stuffing is heated through.

SPECIAL EXTRA:
Assemble as directed, adding ¼ cup KRAFT Shredded Mozzarella Cheese to stuffing mixture before spooning into tomato shells. Sprinkle with ¼ cup KRAFT Grated Parmesan Cheese, then bake as directed.

tuna cakes

PREP: 10 min. | TOTAL: 26 min. (incl. refrigerating) | MAKES: 6 servings.

▶ what you need!

2 cans (6 oz. each) light tuna in water, drained, flaked

1 pkg. (6 oz.) STOVE TOP Stuffing Mix for Chicken

1 cup KRAFT Shredded Mild Cheddar Cheese

¾ cup water

1 carrot, shredded

⅓ cup KRAFT Real Mayo Mayonnaise

2 Tbsp. CLAUSSEN Sweet Pickle Relish

▶ make it!

1.

2.

3.

MIX all ingredients. Refrigerate 10 min. Heat large nonstick skillet sprayed with cooking spray on medium heat.

USE ice cream scoop to add ⅓-cup portions of tuna mixture, in batches, to skillet.

FLATTEN into patties with back of spatula. Cook 6 min. or until golden brown on both sides, carefully turning patties over.

FOR EASIER HANDLING IN THE SKILLET:
Mix all ingredients. Shape into patties as directed. Place in single layer on baking sheet. Refrigerate 1 hour before cooking as directed.

HEALTHY LIVING:
Save 60 calories and 8 grams of fat per serving by preparing with KRAFT 2% Milk Shredded Cheddar Cheese and KRAFT Light Mayo Reduced Fat Mayonnaise.

turkey and stuffing cakes

PREP: 15 min. | TOTAL: 25 min. | MAKES: 8 servings.

▶ what you need!

2 cups leftover prepared STOVE TOP Stuffing Mix, any flavor

2 cups finely chopped leftover cooked turkey

1 cup finely chopped celery

½ cup KRAFT Real Mayo Mayonnaise

½ cup flour

2 Tbsp. GREY POUPON Dijon Mustard

1 egg

1 canned chipotle pepper in adobo sauce, finely chopped

2 Tbsp. oil

½ cup KRAFT Ranch Dressing

▶ make it!

1. **MIX** all ingredients except oil and dressing until well blended. Shape into 8 patties.

2. **COOK** in hot oil in large skillet on medium heat 4 to 5 min. on each side or until golden brown on both sides.

3. **SERVE** with dressing.

   HEALTHY LIVING:
   Save 7 grams of fat per serving by preparing with KRAFT Light Mayo Reduced Fat Mayonnaise.

   NOTE:
   For milder flavor, omit the chipotle pepper. Or for added heat, use more peppers.

VOLUME MEASUREMENTS (dry)

1/8 teaspoon = 0.5 mL
1/4 teaspoon = 1 mL
1/2 teaspoon = 2 mL
3/4 teaspoon = 4 mL
1 teaspoon = 5 mL
1 tablespoon = 15 mL
2 tablespoons = 30 mL
1/4 cup = 60 mL
1/3 cup = 75 mL
1/2 cup = 125 mL
2/3 cup = 150 mL
3/4 cup = 175 mL
1 cup = 250 mL
2 cups = 1 pint = 500 mL
3 cups = 750 mL
4 cups = 1 quart = 1 L

VOLUME MEASUREMENTS (fluid)

1 fluid ounce (2 tablespoons) = 30 mL
4 fluid ounces (1/2 cup) = 125 mL
8 fluid ounces (1 cup) = 250 mL
12 fluid ounces (1 1/2 cups) = 375 mL
16 fluid ounces (2 cups) = 500 mL

WEIGHTS (mass)

1/2 ounce = 15 g
1 ounce = 30 g
3 ounces = 90 g
4 ounces = 120 g
8 ounces = 225 g
10 ounces = 285 g
12 ounces = 360 g
16 ounces = 1 pound = 450 g

DIMENSIONS

1/16 inch = 2 mm
1/8 inch = 3 mm
1/4 inch = 6 mm
1/2 inch = 1.5 cm
3/4 inch = 2 cm
1 inch = 2.5 cm

OVEN TEMPERATURES

250°F = 120°C
275°F = 140°C
300°F = 150°C
325°F = 160°C
350°F = 180°C
375°F = 190°C
400°F = 200°C
425°F = 220°C
450°F = 230°C

BAKING PAN SIZES

Utensil	Size in Inches/Quarts	Metric Volume	Size in Centimeters
Baking or	8×8×2	2 L	20×20×5
Cake Pan	9×9×2	2.5 L	23×23×5
(square or	12×8×2	3 L	30×20×5
rectangular)	13×9×2	3.5 L	33×23×5
Loaf Pan	8×4×3	1.5 L	20×10×7
	9×5×3	2 L	23×13×7
Round Layer	8×1½	1.2 L	20×4
Cake Pan	9×1½	1.5 L	23×4
Pie Plate	8×1¼	750 mL	20×3
	9×1¼	1 L	23×3
Baking Dish	1 quart	1 L	—
or Casserole	1½ quarts	1.5 L	—
	2 quarts	2 L	—